PROOF OF EXISTENCE

Also by Phyllis Becker

How I Learned to Love Jazz

PROOF OF EXISTENCE

Phyllis Becker

POEMS

Scapegoat Press
Kansas City, Missouri

Copyright © 2024 by Phyllis Becker

Cover and book design: Cynthia Beard

Author photo by Colette Waters

Cover and interior art by Toni E. Carpenter: Cover art, "Humanity"; section page for "Migration," "Geometric Shimmers"; section page for "She Can Still Dance," "Tired Feet"; section page for "The Language of Clouds," "Tree"; section page for "Hey, All You Dead People!", "Mask of Colors"; section page for "Hellos and Goodbyes," "Scattered"; section page for "Coming into View," "Yet Another Self."

Additional art courtesy of the author for section "Nelle's Stories," photo of Caroline and Martin; end of book image of African American Civil War Memorial.

Scapegoat Press
P.O. Box 410962
Kansas City, Missouri 64141
www.scapegoatpress.com

ISBN 978-0-9791291-7-9

With deep gratitude for my Aunt Nelle Becker-Slaton, our beloved family historian and storyteller.

Acknowledgments

Thanks to the editors of the following publications where some of the poems in this book previously appeared:

Curating Home: "Coming Upon *Painting for My Dad at the Nelson-Atkins Museum*"
I-70 Review: "Here and There," "Heedless"
KC Art Magazine: "And There You Are Again"
New Letters: "Etta's Body Double"
River Paw Press: "The World Coughs"
The Same: "Meeting Michael Jackson," "Sounds of Being Alive," "Nelle's Stories (I), Passing: Aunt Katherine," "Ancestor Worship," "Filters"
Thorny Locust: "Hot as . . . ," "Life Constricts," "Coming Into View," "It's the Night of the Super Blood Moon," "Ancestor Worship"
Worcester Review and *The Shining Years: Poems about Aging:* "She Can Still Dance"
Whirly Bird: "The Other Side of Windows"

Thank you to my husband, Mark, for his support, not to mention his wonderful meals; Pat for her patient editing; my writing groups, the Diversifiers and Collaborators; and Linda and Ben for their persistent encouragement.

I also want to thank the branches of my family tree, the Beckers, Occomys, Whites, Jones, and Whittakers. Our collective strength is something to behold.

Contents

I
Nelle's Stories
- 13 Around the World in Fitchburg
- 15 Nelle's Stories (I) Passing: Aunt Katherine 1893–1980
- 16 Nelle's Stories (II) Heart Desires: Aunt Ruth July 10, 1891-1945
- 18 Nelle's Stories: Repeating Tales
- 20 Proof of Existence

II
Migration
- 23 CD #2: 8mm Clips from South Dakota, 1957, in Black and White and Color
- 25 Heedless
- 26 The House Across the Street—1969–1975
- 27 Meeting Michael Jackson
- 29 Fleeing to DC, the Chocolate City (CC)
- 31 Breaking the Rules
- 32 30-Year-Old Photo
- 33 Leavenworth National Cemetery, March 13, 2011

III
She Can Still Dance
- 35 Dreaming I Am Sewing
- 36 Etta's Body Double
- 37 She Can Still Dance
- 38 The Other Side of Windows

IV
The Language of Clouds
- 41 Filters
- 43 For Me and for You, Too
- 45 In the Last Year of Your Life
- 46 Coming upon *Painting for My Dad* at the Nelson-Atkins Museum
- 47 How I Knew, How I Know, He's Gone
- 48 The Day after Your Funeral

V
Hey, All You Dead People!

- 51 Ancestor Worship
- 52 While Cleaning Through Your Things
- 53 Eclipses
- 55 Chipped Edges
- 56 Our World Coughs
- 57 Life Constricts
- 58 Hey, All You Dead People!

VI
Hellos and Goodbyes

- 60 Here and There
- 63 Much Has Changed and Much Has Not
- 64 My Cat and My Friend
- 65 Mantra for Sienna at the State Mental Hospital
- 66 The Sounds of Being Alive

VII
Coming into View

- 70 Coming into View
- 72 The Drama of the Charm
- 73 It's the Night of the Super Blood Moon
- 74 Not the Real Deal
- 75 Our invisible kid
- 76 Hot as . . .
- 78 Relativity
- 80 Let the Snow Fall
- 81 Embrace It
- 82 And there you are again
- 84 The Strangeness of Home

- 86 *Notes*
- 88 *Biography*

"The chances of me existing, the chances of anyone existing," she said . . . , "are as small as one against all of the stars, if each star is its own universe."

—Cynthia Odu, 18-year-old Nigerian immigrant,
Kansas City Star, May 10, 2014

I
Nelle's Stories

Martin and Caroline Becker married circa 1850

Around the World in Fitchburg

"Few areas of American genealogy research poses as much of a challenge [as in] the search for African American families."

—Kimberly Powell, ThoughtCO., November 18, 2019

I find Volume 2 of *Around the World in Fitchburg*,
dusty in my parents' basement. The tape
my mother used to cover a tear on the dust jacket
yellows with age. In the book, one sees the world
in the town of Fitchburg, Massachusetts, through the eyes
of immigrants, racial, and ethnic groups. In chapter six,
"A Dream Deferred," I find: *One of the most prominent*
Negro families in the late 1800s was that of the Beckers,
the Beckers of my ancestry—my past, my present.
Aunt Nelle, the family historian, told stories of Martin Becker,
of Fitchburg fame, son of Willem Becker, an African Bushman,
who came to these United States via Surinam, Dutch Guiana,
and took the *Becker* name from a Dutchman for whom he worked.
Martin was a *free Black man* my aunt emphasized,
hearing that I felt free in ways beyond physical.
Martin, a barbershop proprietor, a Civil War soldier, left
his wife Caroline and their four children after the war
for Fanny Young and their three children in South Carolina.
Back to *Around the World of Fitchburg*, Martin's son Charles
ran a writing school in which he taught penmanship.
In a photo, Charles wears a white wide-brimmed hat, slightly
cocked, a white shirt, tie, dark jacket with a white pocket hanky.
He sits at a table, one hand holding a pen, the other
resting on his cheek. His eyes ironic, his mustache full,
his nose familiar. The photo caption: *Ready for business*.
Martin's other son, Hendrick, conducted Becker's Orchestra,
an all-white band, except for him. A picture shows
him and his band members in formal wear.

Hendrick, in the middle, holds an upright bass.
Before I close this chapter, I find other forebears' names,
marriages, jobs, moves, deaths, births, and then
my aunt and my father appear, colliding
with the edges of my universe, the world as I know it.

Nelle's Stories (I) Passing: Aunt Katherine 1893–1980

Katherine passed as *Princess Reba* on the stage:
tango dancer, cannon fodder in a Coney Island act,
and a psychic tea-leaf reader at Zimmerman's
Bulgaria nightclub in New York City.
Five feet, three inches, with light brown skin,
long dark hair, she joked with her niece that while
dancing at supper clubs with her Italian
partner/lover she'd pass as a Spaniard
or Italian, whatever *suited her fancy*.
Pregnant at seventeen, she left her only child
in the care of her mother, passing
in and out of her relatives' home.
Katherine taught her darker-skinned
niece, Nelle, to call herself an Indian if anyone
asked when Nelle visited her home in the
whites-only apartment building.
Time passed, Katherine's dancer legs
bowed with arthritis. She lived her last days
in the family home in Providence,
reading the tea leaves for her visiting niece.
When Katherine died, people talked:
Was she feckless or brave? Nelle fondly
remembered visiting Aunt Katherine,
aka *Princess Reba*, in her New York apartment
and hearing tales of worlds where she would never pass.

Nelle's Stories (II) Heart Desires: Aunt Ruth July 10, 1891-1945

Aunt Ruth was loyal and faithful, it was said
(as was Ruth in the Good Book).
Some compared Ruth to her sister Katherine,
a dancer and crystal-ball reader.
Ruth steadfastly studied overcoming
barriers for Blacks to become a nurse.
Ruth never married.
She'd take her niece and nephew
to pray over sick parishioners,
wash dishes, read a Bible verse,
or a selected poem.
A stern babysitter, she warned
her charges to behave.
In 1928, at age thirty-six,
she fulfilled her heart's desire
to minister in Monrovia, Liberia.
Her nephew, who later became a doctor,
aspired to go to Africa like his aunt.
Her mother lamented her leaving.
On October 31, 1931, the Providence,
Rhode Island, *Afro American* noted
that the Missionary Society of the Pond
Street Free Baptist Church sent
a Christmas barrel to Ruth in Africa.
When she returned home she brought
cocoa beans, trinkets, woven blankets,
and enthralled and horrified her nieces
and nephews with stories about the
Firestone Corporation selling liquor labeled
Jesus Tears to the native rubber workers
and about the (secret and exclusive) Leopard Society

of Monrovia who, in a once-a-year ritual, scared
the villagers to stay inside because, if caught,
their hearts would be cut out for the good of the tribe.
Her nephew did well, started a thriving practice,
but never made it to Africa.

Nelle's Stories: Repeating Tales

As told by my Aunt Nelle,
Esther, my great-great-great-grandmother,
an enslaved person and seamstress,
was freed by her master. Her husband Francis was not.
Francis Jr., born in 1830, was not Sr.'s biological son.
Everyone knew his father was the plantation owner.
Francis Jr. was a carpenter and musician
who played five instruments.

A friend of one of my white relatives
by marriage prods me with questions about
why *my people* would claim Obama because
he wasn't Black but half white. Like Francis Jr.,
my white husband is a carpenter. One night at a bar,
while listening to jazz (we were dating then), a drunk
acquaintance leaned over to my soon-to-be husband
and said, "You're not going to marry her, are you?"
We call these our multicultural moments and laugh.

Francis Jr. moved North, married three times.
One of Francis's daughters, Nellie
(my Aunt's grandmother and namesake)
married Walter. Walter's mother, Catherine,
was sent away to work in a white household
when she was a child (like many Black children).
At thirteen, Catherine blacked out the night her employer
came into her bedroom. His wife put her out
when she told them she was pregnant.
Walter was later heard to bitterly say,
She was put out in the dead of winter.

A picture of Catherine, with *high cheekbones*
and lovely eyes, hung in my Aunt Nelle's grandparent's
bedroom (and as the story goes), Aunt Nelle
at age five overhead the story of Catherine,
her great-grandmother, and Aunt Nelle said
to her grandfather, Walter, "Grandpa, I didn't know
you had a white father," and was promptly slapped.
Her grandmother held her, whispered to her,
You mustn't repeat tales.

When my husband and I got married,
there were whispers, comments, curiosity,
and other multicultural moments.
We cried and held hands when Obama won;
we cried and laughed because we had a choice.
We married, late, as they say, dashing my father's
hope of passing on the family name, and
sometimes we are dismayed we have no children,
but we mostly enjoy the freedom.

Proof of Existence

"In May 1863, the Government established the Bureau of Colored
Troops to manage the burgeoning numbers of black soldiers."
—Budge Weidman, "Preserving the Legacy of United States
Colored Troops," National Archives

Bumping along in the family-reunion bus
to the memorial, we are lit by laughter,
the hum of conversations. Connecting the dots
of our family history, we revel in the coming home
of commonalities and the softening of edges
of distances, differences, disconnections.
It feels urgent, as if this could be the last time
we will see each other again due to circumstance,
or brutal fate, the natural progression of our legacy.
We pull up to the African American Civil War Memorial,
young and old run, walk fast to the Memorial
to confirm the names of our ancestors:
Theodore J. Becker, 54th Regiment, Massachusetts,
hospital steward (Colored),
Martin Becker, 55th Regiment, Massachusetts
Infantry Company B (Colored).
We hastily tear papers, lay them over
the raised letters of their names, and create a relief
to show proof of their and our existence.

II

Migration

CD #2: 8mm Clips from South Dakota, 1957, in Black and White and Color

Clip 1 (black & white)

Black-and-white images flicker, my mother
holds me, I am one year old. Long-legged, she wears
cotton shorts and a plaid sleeveless top. She is fair-skinned;
her curly, brunet hair droops in the heat. She stands in front
of a white clapboard house in Hot Springs, South Dakota.
*She would later tell me how sad she was there, how she hated
how the Indians were treated. How she missed her mother.*
The clip rolls on. I sit on my mother's hip.
She stares down the road.

Clip 2 (color)

My father's sister's family drives through the Badlands from LA to visit
*(a long way from Putnam Avenue, Brooklyn, New York,
where my parents and aunt grew up).*
My cousin, braids festooned with red bows, scampers across
the creek rocks and boulders. My sister, thirteen, wears saddle shoes,
black Capris, a white sleeveless shirt, cat glasses, and no smile.
As the oldest, she took care of me when my mother couldn't.
The water rolls and froths in the creek.

Clip 3 (color)

My oldest brother climbs a fence, his eyes merry. My younger
brother follows him up to see where the buffalo roam.
Window scenes from the car as it drives up the mountains.
*The same car we crash a few months later on our way to our new home
in Kansas. My brother broke his leg. My mother ended up in the hospital.*
The car stops at a lookout station. My dad and the others
peer at the valleys and hills. Rocks balance precariously.

Clip 4 (black & white)

The Plymouth Belvedere rolls to a stop in front of the house.
Everyone clambers out of the car. My dad looks out of place
in his business clothes. The kids play in the yard. The adults
move to the shade under the trees. My mother and I sit on the porch.
*In recurring dreams (after my mother died) she does not get a long
illness; she lives on her own, gives me unasked-for advice.*
She and I flicker in the grainy image.
She holds me on her hip, her mouth at my ear,
telling me something important.

Heedless

Warned about the deadly rattle of the tail
of the snake—*watch out, don't step on it*—
we kids formed a semi-circle, looking down in awe
at the skin of the rattler, the way we looked down
at my brother, who fell out of the tree we climbed.
He lay crumpled and still until he jumped up
and laughed at us. Oh, how I hated him.

In school photos and candids of us
with the neighbrhood kids, we stood out
with our darker skin, nappy hair,
in a universe of young white faces.
This *otherness* whispered about by the adults
still just a neat difference for us.

My brother watched out for his younger siblings.
We ranged far and wide in our small town,
and we did the things of a mother's nightmare.
We put pennies on railroad tracks to smash
and stood on the tracks, running when we heard the train coming,
rummaged through the cast-offs and litter in junkyards,
leaped over drainage ditches, and took day trips walking
to the graveyard, all the way to the highway
to watch the cars rush by.

In one of our favorite games, we abandoned
our shoes in the fields, heedless of rusty nails, and wrapped
our arms around each others' shoulders, marched to the tune
of a one-line song we made up and belted at the top of our lungs:
barefooted buddies, barefooted buddies, barefooted buddies . . . .

The House Across the Street—1969–1975

We ripped and tore through the neighborhood
streets, the woods, backyards, through front and
back doors, and the culvert the creek ran through.
We were one of two Black families on the block.

As each year passed, the white kids
disappeared—their parents plucked them up,
moved them farther west—along with their pets
and station wagons we waved to as they passed by.

The Kirkpatricks from across the street the last to go.
No more Gary to run us girls off from the boys' cave
they built in the woods. No more birthday parties
with Pam, no invites to their new homes.

The nieghborhood and the houses changed colors
as new families filled the homes. Different cars
in the driveways—Oldsmobiles, a Volkswagon—and there
were Junior, KC, Linda, and Vanessa to play with.

And like the trees and shrubs, we filled out and grew tall.
The house across the street went up for sale again.
Vanessa and I smoked Newport Smooths behind the empty
house where the backyard met the woods and creek.

Meeting Michael Jackson

During his *ABC* days,
in the Jackson 5,
his skin still mocha brown,
his nostrils could flare.
Teens and preteens,
we put in dibs on our favorite
Jackson boy and allowed no
changing or two-timing.
My pick? Tito, by default.
Michael, Marlon, and Jermaine
already quickly chosen by my sister
and friends. Jackie was too old.
When we got the word we were going
to meet them, we thought
anything was possible.

We stepped out of the elevator,
and there was Michael—in the hallway,
in a big apple cap, knocking hard rolls
(like golf balls) from a room-service
tray with an umbrella.
We didn't care at the time
that he didn't even look at us.
In their room, they ate
Gates Bar-B-Q.
There were others in the room.
We stepped up for introductions.

And now it's all a blur
I've pieced together from photos.
My sister, coy, doe-eyed,
stood next to Michael, he

a foot and a half shorter than her.
Our next-door neighbor smiling
ear to ear, shoulder to shoulder with Marlon.
I felt excited but deflated
standing next to Tito in a group shot.
He wore a large-brimmed hat
and stood on my right, little Michael
and a neighbor boy in the front row.
I did not smile, my Afro
the largest in the room
as we posed and posed.

Fleeing to DC, the Chocolate City (CC)

> "Hey, uh, we didn't get our forty acres and a mule
> But we did get you, CC, heh, yeah."
> —"Chocolate City," Parliament

In 1974 I unpacked my bags at Howard University,
my brothers', father's and uncle's alma mater,
and dunked myself into Chocolate City,
the hubbub of DC politics and Black culture.
(Back then, seven out of ten Washington DCers were Black
and whites had moved to the suburbs en masse at the end of WW II).
As I packed my bag in our ranch-style home in suburban
Kansas City, Kansas, where my East Coast parents bought
their dream home in the Midwest for a price, one of three Black
families who integrated the neighborhood, tipping it into white flight.
The seventies: house parties, bell bottoms, Afros,
platform shoes, Black Power, and funk all the rage.
The Jackson 5, War, Ohio Players, and Earth, Wind & Fire played
on the *SOOOUL TRAAAIN* on the TV
as my busy, stressed mom stopped vacuuming and danced
with my brother, sister, and me in our own *Soul Train* line.
I'd sit in my bedroom and dream of leaving Kansas.
I thought I could retrace my parents' steps,
flee the suburbs, leave the mowed lawns, big backyards,
two-car garages, and head back east for the big cities.
And CC was all that: marches, presidential elections,
monuments, music, and soul brothers and sisters.
And after late nights in the books, partying, and rounds
of Rise and Fly spades, I would find myself in
the mirror in my small dorm room picking my 'fro,
turning my head left to right, studying myself.

Breaking the Rules

My six-year-old niece asks me
why I don't have any children,
says I would be a good mommy.
She makes up a story, a book titled
Auntie Phyllis and My Four Friends.
We illustrate it with watercolors.
My father always said I was like
Aunt Ruth, a missionary
in Africa, and he said my sister was
like Aunt Katherine, a dancer.
A photo shows Aunt Katherine
in a chiffon dress, turban, hand
on a crystal ball. In another Aunt Ruth
stands stiff, unsmiling, looking
straight at the camera.
At fifteen, I dreamed of being
single in a swank apartment drinking
cocktails and entertaining friends.
Marriage came later in my crystal ball.
I now seek out sepia pictures of my aunts.
I am drawn to the fierce look in Aunt Ruth's eyes,
Aunt Katherine's dreamy gaze.
I understand feeling old before
you're old, and on the days I don't
feel old, I feel young, the heroine
in a watercolor adventure
in my niece's book,
breaking all the rules.

30-Year-Old Photo

In a box, taped shut from a previous move,
in the back of the closet, in an envelope unopened,
I find a black-and-white photo. *Is that me?*
It is—but disconnected by space and time
from memory, or feeling.
Thin arms akimbo, long legs in sharp angles.
She sits atop a stone porch,
fringed in lady ferns and hostas.
Her dark hair wild, woolly, her eyes large, dark,
and wide open, she looks into the camera, seeing
and unseeing, unknowing, unaware
of the box that will close around her.
I read the photo like text. I feel tilted,
distanced, but reunited to this intimate
stranger bathed in slanted shadows.

LEAVENWORTH NATIONAL CEMETERY, MARCH 13, 2011

Running through the cemetery at night
was a childhood dare you claimed
you took, but I have my doubts.
At night, did you stare through your
third-floor window at the glowing white tombs
that seemed to undulate on the hills under
a pie moon during a hot Midwestern summer,
hot enough for your little brother
to get in trouble for cooking goose eggs
on the sidewalks behind our old white house?
While looking out the window in your twilight-lit room,
did you dream of the coast where you'd eventually
escape to, leaving behind sisters and a brother
you'd pulled pranks on and taught the boogaloo?
Thinking of the calm Pacific, did your mind cool?
Did you see yourself kayaking, riding gentle waves?
I bet you never once, while looking through
that window, dreamed of seeing your sister
and a brother-in-law you'd never met walking
to section 44, row 31, site 41 on the day and month
of your birth, peering past rolling hills of white tombs
to a white house, pointing to a third-floor window,
stopping to stand in front of a tomb etched with
your name and *Beloved By All*.

III

She Can Still Dance

Peytonia "Toni" Becker circa 1941

Dreaming I Am Sewing

For her sweet sixteenth
my mother sewed her dress:
a long red, velvet skirt and a short top
with puffy sleeves. She wore it as she leaned
against a brick wall in a black-and-white photo.
Chin down, eyes wide, eyebrows raised,
she looked smoking smart like Lena Horne
or Lauren Bacall. She learned to sew
from her philandering father, a tailor.
As an adult, she barely spoke to him
but carried on the craft, creating her designs,
fixing too big or too small finds, repeatedly
re-upholstering the same furniture set for decades,
each new cover a chance to reinvent the living room
from brocade to stripes, to pastels.
After her mother died, her father moved in
with his other family, and my mother taught
my sister and me how to sew. McCall's patterns,
wild prints, and colorful solid fabrics
filled the living-room floor as we listened
and learned. She was happy then. She could thread
any needle, darn a sock, sew a costume,
make zig-zag stitches straight when she was strong.
My mother didn't go to her father's funeral,
and my brother, sister, and I only met him
once before he died, arriving by cab
from our hotel to his New York City walk-up
where he lived with his second wife.
We sat wedged between our parents
on a small overstuffed couch
before I understood how patterns
can repeat, and seams can tear beyond repair.

Etta's Body Double

Before leaving for the Etta James show,
I helped Mom dress in her best black attire:
signature turban and sparkly earrings.
We loved Etta. We'd listen to her sing
before our Sunday meals, Mom and Dad
reminiscing. When we got to the show,
Etta's voice still boomed strong and clear.
Etta dressed in black, and so much smaller, petite
compared to her younger days,
her light skin powdered, almost like a geisha's.
Her gyrations were brazen and raunchy,
almost too raunchy. She made us laugh
in raw recognition. Mom didn't need
a wheelchair all the time, but we kept her close,
to keep her steady, as she snapped her fingers,
swayed to the music. The band seemed
to hover over Etta, too, watching
her erratic/erotic moves making sure she didn't
misstep as she darted across the stage and sang
"Sunday Kind of Love," "All I Could Do Was Cry,"
and the perennial wedding favorite, "At Last."
The energy pulsed as the show ended.
People were still dancing, smiling, and someone
almost knocked me down, and I thought, how rude,
but then she gave Mom a hug, and what I did not know
at first, was that the adoring crowd thought my mother
was Etta mingling with the crowd. And Mom,
with us at her side, as we left the show,
danced down the aisle like it was a red carpet.
She smiled and waved at anyone who
smiled and waved at her—
she and Etta one, fair-skinned and sassy,
dressed in black and more than beautiful.

She Can Still Dance

The couple remembers music
better than their grandkids' names.
He knows the rhythm, the style,
the artist, the barroom,
and the table where they sat,
tapping feet to the latest jazz tunes.
Now, she can barely walk,
but she can still dance.
Her feet can follow
but not her mind.
Her mind is a rolling brownout,
shutting down one grid at a time.
Nonetheless, he still plays
their music, and though
the damage done
cannot be undone,
some words to a song struggle
to her lips, if not the words,
a melody, a moment of perfect peace
as the Duke plays or Ella sings
"The Nearness of You,"
and if not a melody to hum,
a foot to tap, hands to clap,
if not a clap or tap,
a smile,
for awhile.

The Other Side of Windows

"I little dreamed how much I'd give now, if I could,
for one scowl and a word of discouragement."
—Carl Bettis, "Time Wears All Things Smooth"

From under her full-brimmed hat,
a bit of a smile, a sideways glance
that makes you wonder,
as when passing an almost closed window.
She wears a wrap dress, chunky heels,
somewhere in Brooklyn, circa 1944.

Her son peers through the windshield
between the wiper swipes of driving rains
on his way eastward—home.
After the rains, the mist and clouds
look like smoke, like the earth
had been doused after a big fire.

Her time passes now
in front of windows. He sits next
to her, flipping through decades of photos;
they stop at one of her in a wide-brimmed hat.
He talks in his loud voice,
trying to get a rise,

but she only smiles, mostly silent,
watches squirrels, birds, shadows,
rustling leaves, his car passing by
when he goes. He tries to spot her
in her window but can't see in.

IV

The Language of Clouds

Filters

Sometimes you have to go home.
And you find the bits, pieces, chunks
of you left behind—with your old grade card,
which your teacher wrote on in lovely penmanship
about how smart you were, but quiet (too quiet?)—
and artwork through the years: clay ashtrays,
an abstract painting you don't remember
and would not claim but for your signature.

Death makes everything immediate.
And you are there again; right now, the lid
closes on your mother's casket, and the grandkids
burst into tears, and you feel as if the lid is closing
on you as if an invisible sheet were coming down over you,
your father and siblings. Your family huddles; you feel their
body heat, smell their perfume and sweat, hear quiet sobs
that throb through you as the lid drops down,
and it's as if you all are being shrink-wrapped.

At thirteen, your world was the expanse of your bed
with the groovy psychedelic bedspread
in your room with yellow walls and shag carpet.
Your girlfriends would knock on the door, and as your mother
let them in, they were polite; your dad would barely lift
his head from the TV. You'd hurry them into your room. They'd
giggle, pose like adults they'd soon become, and jump on the bed.
The stories of your collective lives spill across the world
of your old bedspread you now pull out of the dusty trunk
in your parent's garage.

War sounds come through the car radio as you leave your father's house.
You've boxed, vacuumed, fed him, drunk beer, watched TV, and discussed
the picture on the wall, which has hung there your whole life,
and in your father's childhood home. You're beyond exhausted,
and the trunk of your car is stuffed with mementos
of your mother and the backlog of your childhood.
On the radio, the music of the Cellist of Baghdad*
sifts and filters through your racing mind,
the strains he played amid the rubble and ash
after recent bombings fill you up like a hot air balloon.

For Me and for You, Too

The horn player/dancer/singer/
one hell of guy croons
"What a Wonderful World."
The brothers, in their late eighties,
get to the bar on a late afternoon,
(*skies of blue and white clouds, too*)
commandeer the best table,
riff off each other, laugh,
and tell jokes only they get.
They catch up after years apart,
one on the West Coast, the other
in the Midwest. Their last visit
was in LA at their sister's
funeral, which they don't
mention, nor the recent death of a wife,
infirmities, bills piling up
—just not their style.
They nod their heads and dap fists
 with those who pass by.
Their grown children (age fifty plus) arrive late.
Standing room only. The younger
brother leans on his cane,
tells "the kids" what he's learned:
the waitresses' names, the history
of the bar, and he lets them
know that the performer, who just
got married, is fantastic.
The children find a nearby table,
do their own catching up,
keep a watchful eye.
They rehash stories.
The trumpet squeals, blows old
grudges and sins away.

The performer taps deftly down
the bar top, he and the world
framed by floor-to-ceiling
windows, where all can see
(*the bright blessed day* . . .
dark sacred night).
They order another round,
raise glasses to toast as the brothers
unwind the years.

In the Last Year of Your Life

Our heads were often in the clouds,
so much to be said; instead on our drives
together on highways, and turns down
side streets, you'd say, *Look at the clouds*,
as we watched gray-tinged nimbus clouds roll in.
We thought them beautiful, sometimes angry. *Look there*,
we'd say as we crossed from Kansas to Missouri into pillowy
white clouds. Striated clouds made you sad, thoughtful.
So many things spoken in the language of clouds about
things collected, neglected, discarded, found, and lost.
Coming over the bridge on our way back,
you reminded me, *Look at the clouds*, you of good
fortune and good times, you child prodigy,
child of divorce, child of racism and abuse.
Look, you said, until blue skies stilled us into silence.

Coming Upon *Painting for My Dad* at the Nelson-Atkins Museum

> "I, too, stand on the edge of it with a prayer lamp."
> —Noah Davis

Dad's back is to us.
We hunger to see more of him.
His shoulders round slightly, head bows.
He stands in the cavity of a cave
in his dad jeans and slightly large polo.
The insides of the cave's brown rocky walls
form a U-shape, and above, below, and around him is the universe.
The backs of his dark brown arms and Afro
are outlined by the light of the prayer lamp he holds.
He's on the verge of stepping off.
He is blackness and stars.

How I Knew, How I Know, He's Gone

The house was too quiet
(just like I'd imagined it would be),
the hum of the air conditioner too loud.
I called his name—he did not answer.
He was in the middle of the bed.
He always slept on the left side.

The house feels heavy with him
in his absence.
No calls in the middle of the night.
In each of his suit jackets,
we find a handkerchief, two toothpicks,
breath mints.
No one sits in his easy chair.

The Day after Your Funeral

We roll out of bed gelatinous, amoeba-like onto the front porch,
reconstitute our forms and settle comfortably into our broken selves.
We are held by the heat of a hot-ass Midwest summer,
the grass, trees, flowers, sky, and sunlight blur into impressionistic
greens, blues, yellows. Our nephew from out of town joins us
for coffee and silence. His watchful eyes are kind.
Neighbors walk their dogs, mow the grass.
The leaves of the trees form a canopy.
The sweet, heavy odor of green* soothes us.
A cousin and her husband bring bottles
of specially selected wines. Corks pop.
We drink the long day, make toasts, laugh, tear up,
eat cheese, crackers, and fruit. Ants take over the crumbs.
The cousins leave in a flurry of hugs, kisses, and promises.
The nephew retreats into the house.
We sit as the day slips away.
The thrum of the peepers and cicadas surrounds us,
and we are shadows among shadows.

V

Hey, All You Dead People!

Ancestor Worship

I talk to my dead brother,
on occasion.
Yet his strong presence is quiet lately.
As I sleep, a dead friend's face peeks
out of the darkness of a dream
(about my ill mother),
like the moon in mid-eclipse.
At a certain point, we know
we are just a "renter,"
and there's no earthly foundation,
no home, and the story of
you and me will be told
by the children we know
as they grow old,
and in their quiet moments,
and troubled dreams
they will talk to us.
As first light breaks, I wake
whispering, whimpering to the air.

While Cleaning Through Your Things

Found a slip of paper
with your usual small lettering,
the handwriting just starting
to spider.
At the top of the list
a balance of 7,227.20:
July 23/ 97—Loan to Doris—200.00.
Oct. 14 /97—Wedding Gift Elaine—100.00.
A total line for 1997 with no total.
Dec.98—Earl 200.00.
The price of an opal ring you gave
to me but listed for my sister.
Amer. Red Cross 100.00—Mar 29/98.
Then the writing shrinks, fades, spikes—
listings of my brothers and sisters
and the number of grandkids,
checks and cross-outs,
debts not paid,
numbers not adding up.

Eclipses

Grimace/Smile

We gather in the best part of the yard
of the apartment building with two other neighbors
whose paths we would normally never cross:
the retired vet recovering from a heart attack
with Luna, his terrier pup, and a woman from the Ozarks
in the building across the street. The crescents made by gaps
in the leaves look like smiles, grimaces.

Moon Crossing the Sun

My allergies overcome me from handling and sorting moldy, dusty
papers, the last of the boxes from my parents' home.
It's painful, the slow deciding of what papers to keep, throw out.
Impatient, I want to throw it all out but don't.
I pack a box of clothes to send to my brother,
keep notes my father saved from my mother for my sister,
But what to do, what to do with the hundreds of photos?

Totality

We chit chat with our newly discovered neighbors.
We check the sky with our protective glasses.
The moon takes bites out of the sun.
My husband and I hold hands, in awe, as bright
day suddenly turns twilight, then dark, and the sounds
of frogs, cicadas rise like background music cued in a movie.

Path of the Eclipse

An artist friend comes over to look at Mom's and Dad's art.
We drink bourbon in the middle of the day.
She carefully inspects their collection,
tells me their choices reflect our family history

and "do not," she said, "do not ever sell the painting
that hung in your father's childhood home before he was born."

Uncovered

Totality over, the moon moves on its path,
inch by inch, revealing the sun, and our moment
with the neighbors ends. They walk down different
paths home. We wave. The vet grimaces as he leans
on his cane. His pup scampers ahead. We turn
towards our place. I think about my parents'
things and what else I might uncover.
I relax as the din of wildlife subsides.

Chipped Edges

After my mother died, I noticed chips
on so many of her things: bowls, plates,
the cups of her beautiful china.
I placed her clay sculpture of a woman's profile
toward the wall to hide the side where the nose is chipped.
These chips made me angry. I wonder how this damage
came to be. Was it the grandchildren running wild
through the house, my dad, unaware and knocking
things over, or a careless cleaning lady?
It seemed a referendum of her life.
Today, I pull out bowls in my cupboard:
a wedding gift and an old bowl of my husband's aunt.
They are chipped, and a quick inventory finds more chips.
I curse myself as I can blame no one else, my only excuse the rush
of my too-busy life, the impatient putting away of things.
I dust one of the bowls of Mother's that is still perfect,
oblong-shaped with extravagant curved arms.
The light filters through the amber glass
of this piece of art passed on to me with her other things,
and I know with the luxury of time comes chipped edges.

Our World Coughs

As if day turned into night in the middle
of the afternoon like a full eclipse,
we now find ourselves sheltering in place.
Today, the thunder and lightning
roll and crack like huge bowling balls.
The sounds somehow soothe, match my mood.
I lie in bed and listen, go inward
and back to a time sewing with my mother—
each pattern, each chosen fabric cut through
my eighth-grade anguish. And with my hair freed
from chemicals, my buoyant 'fro, and the beautiful
clothes I sewed to fit my tall, skinny frame,
I was altered. Now, fifty years later,
my mother alive only in dreams,
I rouse at 5:00 a.m., and I hear
(what I now call) *my birds* urgently chirping
me out of my waking despair.
Our world coughs, and we have nowhere
to run, nowhere to go, yet it is a new day.
I have bed hair, food to eat, clothes that fit,
I mark each breath.

Life Constricts

Money is tight.
Eyes can't see to drive at night.
Life constricts.

Constraint is noble.
Time is limited.
The family circle tightens.

Memories are thick.
Fruit is sweeter
to the taste.

Old bones move slowly.
Ghosts leave their haunts.
Thoughts tumble.

Hey, All You Dead People!

Why have you come back?
(Grief is not grief—it's the wide-eyed
stare of the haunted.)
Drink, food, sex, but I still cannot escape
the inescapable. You've all come to live in me
and taken squatter's rights.
I have learned to not fight you,
and you have become quieter,
less haunty-ish, more hush than howl.
Now, it's more like a co-existence,
possession without resistance.
Hey there, you, yes you hiding behind my rib cage,
and you controlling my fingers, my script.
And you in my head, my heart
and behind my eyes. You, my friends, keeping
tabs on me and my lovely, lonely life.

VI

Hellos and Goodbyes

Here and There

> You'll turn toward the window
> (catching a reflection
> you'll see right through)
> and watch hurricanes rip clouds
> across a bone-white moon,
> thin as a clipped fingernail.
>
> —Phil Miller, "Great Winds, Great Rain"

Grimy from dust after the
final packing of pictures and the last
of the bric-a-brac from your garage sale,
in Kansas City, we sit exhausted with you and
Nancy on the couch you got from your mother.

Later, you both stand on your porch
shoulder to shoulder, smile, and wave bye.
The city lights fan out around us
as we drive away from your old house,
the moon a clipped nail in the sky.

Months later, we drive highways
following winding roads through
the mountains, reading the landscape
and map of Pennsylvania, taking us
us to your new home in Mount Union.

And we sit on your mother's couch
in rooms with an old European feel,
marveling at how your old things
look new, and the big ball of a moon
suspended between the hills.

But now, we leave your old home
no longer yours. We watch your receding,

waving figures as we drive the familiar curves
of roads we won't need to travel anymore,
but will on occasion be drawn to,

even after we arrive and turn excitedly
into the back alley of your new home,
and we are there and here, like the moon,
as you both stand shoulder to shoulder, smiling,
waving hellos and goodbyes.

Much Has Changed and Much Has Not

Outside the hotel in St. Johnsbury,
Vermont, we sit and gaze at the hills, happy
to escape the clutter of our life. Our eyes close.
We listen to the stiff breeze dancing with
the leaves, which takes away our churning.
We drive through town. The sumac has turned red,
Our host/friend shows us the closed factories.
We buy carrots at the market.
Several big brown leaves scutter across our path
while he talks of the young people leaving town.
The eighteenth-century corner building is still grand
but dingy with loose bricks. People hang out open
windows to watch the parade we come upon.
Children pick up candy from the street, tossed to them
by the grand marshal. It's cloudy. Rain threatens
as we jump into the car. The radio drones bad news.
A decade has passed since we have seen our friend.
Much has changed, and much has not.
We drink martinis (like we used to)
except now he stirs and adds a lemon peel.
We toast to past happy hours.
The mountain air and gin levitate us.
Old-timey jazz plays as we eat dinner, with peppers
and greens from his garden. We get lost
going back to the hotel. We see no deer or moose,
only a fox caught in headlights.
On our last day, we draw back to the hills
behind the hotel, to the rustling leaves
and discover a small waterfall, listen to the splash,
gurgle, and shushing of the creek, rushing
down a ravine, next to an abandoned paper mill.

My Cat and My Friend

Janice loved my cat, Bibsy; she would stroke
his head, say they were alike.
Both had brutal early lives, exposed
to the cruelties of an indifferent world.
Yet they survived, even thrived.
Both had presence, style—
Bibs with his big head, white bibbed
chest, thick tail, and melodious mews,
and Janice with her bright colors, headbands,
sparkly costume jewelry, and wild, thick hair.
But they differed: everyone loved Bibs,
your lap his domain. Bibs kept his areas tidy,
indoors or out, his purr an open
invitation for a pet. Janice could be prickly,
anxious in conversation, quick to defense,
her piles of things a barrier—
her delicate teacups, her intricate artwork,
decades of magazines, ornate crosses,
chandeliers, chimes. And the bats: bat hats,
stuffed-animal bats, bat photos, hanging bats
filled every crook and crevice,
hallway, floor, and room in her small apartment.
There was great beauty and method to her madness
(she might have said with a laugh).
Given that they shouldn't have made it so far in life,
it was a surprise when they died (only weeks apart).
I sometimes think I hear Bibs meowing
and find myself saying Janice's favorite line:
Bats sure are sweet, aren't they?

Mantra for Sienna at the State Mental Hospital

Once again, reports from staff trend grim.
They talk softly, stand alert, tense, waiting.
You pace the room, ready to explode

I see you busting down doors.
I see you rebuking staff, proxies for your abusers:
your stepfather, the boy down the street,
your mother's boyfriends.

I see you jerking, scratching, squirming,
tumbling as if you could shed
them like a second skin.

I see the fear in your eyes,
which you tuck away in a hard glare, keep hidden
behind the slashes on your arms,
the tattoos, the piercings.

I hear your words gushing, splattering
the cinderblock walls of your brightly
painted room until you are all screamed out.

I see you in your dreams as you battle.
I see the walls of your institutions
begin to crumble.

I see you.

The Sounds of Being Alive

I have always been a morning person,
liked the time before all the squabbles,
skirmishes of the day ensued, the time for gearing up
and sometimes humming, "What a Difference
a Day Makes," Dinah Washington's version. Hope lived
in the morning. Evening was the beginning of the end.

It's been the losses. The losses of friendships,
of time (the daily disappointments over things not done),
or loss with a capital *D*: the Death of a parent, dear friend,
a pet, and the never-ending blitzes of petite insults, crooked
comments, or the barely veiled conflicts masking anger,
and all that has turned me off the illusions of morning.

I keep repeating things: stories, sayings, mutterings.
Here I go again, writing about what a now-dead friend told
me after a bad bout in the hospital, almost whispering
(as if he might be caught) on a phone thousands
of miles away, saying: "I've got it all figured out,"
but a nurse or doctor arrived, and he hung up
before he could tell me what *it* was.

I don't have *it* figured out. We come into this world
bloody, and dying is not easy. I've left pieces of myself
in places and have not reclaimed them. I am tired of those
who blithely believe in miracles (and now mornings)
and can't look at the hard truth of day and still be kind.

Dusk comes—part day, part night, the time to accept what I don't
know and what I've lost. The sun slips away and my
un-worked-for dreams. The night buzzes. Dogs bark warnings.

I listen to the clanking, thumping, bumping, tinkering of my husband in the kitchen—sounds that annoyed me are now the sounds I love, the sounds of being alive.

VII

Coming into View

Coming Into View

You turn left; the park is distant, hazy.
You can't tell if it is a young or old
man huddled on the bench with a hood over
his head, or a trash bag filled with leaves.
You wonder why it is that all you see
are the shadows, crevices
and the way the park nestles
as if in the bottom of a bowl with no easy exits?
You watch a girl approach the park.
She's wearing a halter top and shorts,
seems so young and unaware.

Where have you forgotten you've walked,
cut off from original sins until your world
resembles a carnival mirror and while coming
upon a park, hazy and distant,
you walk back to a day, decades ago,
to a park where a stranger grabbed you
or an earlier park when you swung on a swing, your legs
pumping hard as your young and beautiful mother
sat on a bench looking off somewhere
to a place you could not see.

The glare of the sun is unforgiving.
You change lanes, check the rearview,
unprepared for a curve in the road;
you swing wide as the park comes into view.
Shadows give way to green lawns
and a path between trees and bushes,
the girl has entered into and disappeared.

The Drama of the Charm

A group of hummingbirds is called a charm.

Front Porch

Hummingbirds triple
at our feeder as summer ends--
migratory instinct. While we sit on the porch
they zoom by our heads. Sometimes the charm's
incessant chatting/chitting, dipping, diving,
near collisions, and deflecting maneuvers
to guard one feeder—while nearby feeders
are birdless—plays on my nerves, sets my teeth
to grind, stipples my anxiety, makes me jumpy.
Seven months into the pandemic and we are still healthy.
The church youth drum and dance marching band
spread out to practice in the church parking lot.
November lurks in the near future.

Back porch

A cold snap thins the charm. We sip cocktails,
happy to be in each other's company
after a hard so-glad-we-have-work day.
I change the backyard feeder, go to hang it on its hook.
A buzzing at my ear stills me. A hummingbird hovers
a foot away, pivots and turns in place in front of my face.
I say hello, thanks for visiting, but not out loud.
The rat-tat-tat and thump, thump, thump
of the drum and dance band vibrates
through the neighborhood. The hummingbird zips
away, the wind picks up, and we go inside,
turn off the news about the upcoming elections,
prepare dinner. The drums cease.
The pot of water boils.

It's the Night of the Super Blood Moon

Our feet prop on the porch railing, we sip wine and track
the moon's transitions—it's a rare event. We miss
everything: parties, exhibits, movies. Fatigue or duty
usually trumps, but not tonight. This marbling rusty
globe brings us out and the superstitious, the loonies,
the end-of-the-worlders re-singing their song.

The cats curl around our feet, claim our laps,
knead, purr, lick. It is in their DNA to
maintain us as a part of their pride.
They hiss at other cats we can't see at the porch's perimeter.
Our cats, like us, are well fed, yet still maim and kill.

We try not to squabble over stupid things,
the million mundane chores not done: dishes,
laundry, clutter to be picked up, put away
or worry over debt, fusses with friends,
a suspicious mole. The dull roar of things
in the background of our productive lives.

We wave at neighbors we rarely see.
We peer into the dark to get the best view
and even though supposedly the lucky ones,
we cross our fingers behind our backs as the moon
passes out of the shadows and covers the sun.

Not the Real Deal

I am not a poet, though I pretend to be
I am an imposter. I must pretend to get by.
I hope I am a good pretender

I hope you all think I am a poet.
But I can't ask if I am pulling it off or not
because then you would know

that I am an imposter.
If I am not a poet, then what am I really?
A social worker, one who helps others, but I am not sure

because I am an imposter, i.e., not real.
And if I am not real, my poems are not real,
and maybe, just maybe, you are not who you say you are either,

not a real writer, trucker, nurse, teacher, retiree, student,
citizen, immigrant, president, thief, murderer, addict,
wife, husband, boyfriend, girlfriend, dad, mom, sister, brother,

African, Italian, Korean, Indian, Latino,
Christian, Catholic, Baptist, Muslim, Jewish, Atheist
Democrat, Socialist, Republican, Independent.

If you think about it, or just pretend to,
If we could all agree, one imposter to the other,
maybe we can figure out what's left.

Our Invisible Kid

is the kid we never had whom we bring up on occasion.
And we always start with if we had a kid...
he/she sure would be cute and bright.
We discuss how he/she would go to college.

Their names would be old-fashioned: Nelly or
Augustus to honor our well-loved, dead family
members. And then we argue about our
non-existent child, their temperament, talents.

I say, "We can't even agree on how to raise our cats, much less
a child." You say, "He or she would be loved." And then we go
back and forth on how old they might be right now, and
you make a point on how much money we would not have.

We discuss the joys of parenthood: cuddles, first steps,
and heartbreaks like cancers or the spiral of drugs. Does heartbreak
or joy outweigh the other? We always conclude with blessing our
childlessness and the time we have for each other, friends, and family.

And at night, under covers, when we reach for each other
and our ample middle-aged bellies collide, we laugh—
you say, "I can't get my arms around you
with these bellies," and add, "the size of a small child."

Hot As . . .

"Do you believe there's a hell?"
the evangelical witness in a black suit,
clutching pamphlets asks me
when I open my front door, blasted
by the heat of an afternoon scorcher.
His fellow traveler, also suited and
sweating profusely, looks at me, and a somber child
stands next to him, eyes downcast.
The witness's face droops,
when I say, "Well, not really,"
and think, *although it is hot as . . .*,
and we are in a standoff,
as in Click and Clack's
Stump the Chump. The fellow traveler
steps back, the child looks up at me.
So, the witness asks, "Well, do you
believe in heaven (as if saying,
that if I believe in heaven,
there must be a hell)?"
I don't bite, and he quickly
follows with, "Where do people
go if they don't go to heaven?"
And I wanted to say, "*On this earth,
with you, on this hot as hell day*"
but all I say is, "Well, that's a
little tricky, don't you think
(as if to say not very Christian of ya)?"
which garners a smile
from the somber child.
And the witness asks me,
"What can I pray for you?"
I think there's no sense
in being rude and let's get this over with

and say, "Jobs, the economy,"
and he issues a long prayer to his God
for me to believe in the devil
and hell, so I can go to heaven,
ending the prayer, as if an after
thought with a short missive
to God to *please save the economy*
and walks away as he spots
an unsuspecting chump walking down
the burning sidewalk, beelines for him,
taps him on the shoulder, asks, "Do you . . . ?"
The somber child looks back at me, waves.

Relativity

Researchers at the National Institute of Standards and Technology have demonstrated the farther away from the earth you are, the faster time passes, even on a human scale.

From the top-floor apartment,
she sees beginning snow
that has not yet hit the earth.
She sometimes thinks she sees
crystals forming into great white
flakes, and then the sky suddenly fills
with sheets of flowing lace, descending.

She peers down as the huge flakes
get smaller and smaller,
descend slowly, then faster,
closer to the ground.
Small figures of shoppers and workers
below look up at the blowing snow, glittering
as it intersects the glow of streetlights.

The new day breaks. She sees all covered in snow.
Schools and offices close. The boundary
between street and sidewalk disappears.
Pedestrians and cars exist on the same field.
Snow drifts into untouched piles.
Her face reflects in the window.

Her eyes shimmer like the snow
as groups of stranded workers gleefully
conquer the frozen hill as their friends cheer.
She holds up her arms in victory
with them as they reach the top,
and snow cascades again.

Shadows stripe her face as the day dissolves.
She observes strangers helping strangers
to get cars unstuck, spinning wheels to track.
The streets empty. The snow re-covers the piles,
Large, smooth, illuminated lumps
that slumber like dinosaurs.

LET THE SNOW FALL

in deceptive, pretty
little flakes.
Let the snow fall
faster, harder,
obscure the sky.
Let the snow
blanket us,
cover all our things:
cars, homes,
animals, flags,
patios, lawns, hedges,
roads, our cities, suburbs,
countrysides, and capitals.
Let the snow
bury the day, the weeks,
months, years, decades,
centuries, millennia, eras
in its layers.
Let the snow
bend branches,
outline fences,
define geography.
Let the snow
empty our streets
and fill them with silence.

Embrace It

The relentless gray bitter cold days
The landscape reconfigured under torrents of snow.
The pieces of your life that don't fit.
The ice you can't see that coats everything.

And There You Are Again

Like the morning sun
breaking the edge
of dawn, there are those
moments when the thought
comes to you,
say stopping
at a red light,
during a lull
in the conversation,
in a waking dream:
here I am.
Your heart rises
and you say,
I must remember this.
It's as if you just
got here—
appeared on this earth
at this moment.
But then you are there,
moments pass by
like a line of ants.
Breathing is hard.

A sinking feeling
settles in your gut
that people won't stop
talking, the evening
will never end,
sleep won't come.
But there you are again
waking up,
a lover next to you,

or you are sitting at work,
keyboard under your
fingertips. The day,
the month, the years have gone
and you wonder,
*How did I get here,
and what happened
between here and here?*

The Strangeness of Home

> Time goes by,
> Everything else keeps changing
> —Stephen Sondheim, "Old Friends"

Your work in another town is done,
and you return home after a long absence.
To the same street, the same address, yet

neighbors have moved, their furniture rearranged,
an empty lot where there was once a house.
You are a stranger in your homeland.

You see, as through a kaleidoscope
of relationships shifted. Good friends have divorced;
others do not return calls. They have changed.

In dreams, you almost find the car and the lost keys.
You set out to rediscover the city.
Shops have closed. On the corner, a man screams

and paces, and water still spouts
from the fountain of horses on hind legs.
Just the same, there is something you can't

put your finger on as you merge onto the street;
the diffuse glow of the light of day enfolds you.
You have changed

in this old-new strange landscape
you again call home.

African American Civil War Memorial

Notes

"Nelle's Stories (II) Heart Desires: Aunt Ruth July 10, 1891–1945"
More information about Aunt Ruth is available at https://news.google.com/newspapers?nid=2211&dat=19311031&id=gCYmAAAAIBAJ&sjid=6P0FAAAAIBAJ&pg=2669,5088975&hl=en

"Nelle's Stories: Repeating Tales"
This poem is based in part on the essay written by Nelle Becker Slaton: "The Journey of Biracial Identity" (May 29th, 2009). Quotes in italics are from the essay.

"Proof of Existence"
The demand to join the 54th was so great that another regiment was deemed necessary, hence the 55th Regiment. It should be noted that the great majority of soldiers who volunteered for these units were already free.... The 54th Regiment of Massachusetts lost two-thirds of their officers and half of their troops, was memorably dramatized in the film *Glory*. "Black Soldiers in the U.S. Military During the Civil War," National Archives.

"Dreaming I Am Sewing"
Lines in italics from "Don't Put Up My Thread And Needle" by Emily Dickinson

"Filters"
*"The renowned conductor of the Iraqi National Symphony Orchestra has been appearing at the sites of explosions across Baghdad. Just hours after attacks.... For him, this combination of music and place has become a form of resistance, something he told *Morning Edition* when the show reached him at home in Baghdad." —NPR Radio

"For Me and for You, Too"
*"What a Wonderful World," lyrics by Louis Armstrong

"Coming upon *Painting for My Dad* at the Nelson-Atkins Museum"
Painting for My Dad by Noah Davis was inspired by his father who had died. The artist died four years later at the age of thirty-two.

"The Day after Your Funeral"
*From "Odor of Green " by Phil Miller

"Ancestor Worship"
Ancestor worship is based on the belief that the spirits of the dead continue to dwell in the natural world and have the power to influence the fortune and fate of the living. Ancestor worship has been found in various parts of the world and in diverse cultures.

The following poems are based on stories or essays that my Aunt Nelle wrote about our family and ancestors based on her personal experience and research. Each poem is followed by the title of the essay.

Poem, "Nelle's Stories (I) Passing: Aunt Katherine 1893 – 1980."

Essay, "Aunt Katherine" by Nelle Becker Slaton, Ph.D.

Poem, "Nelle's Stories (II) Heart Desires: Aunt Ruth July 10, 1891-1945."

Essay, "Aunt Ruth" by Nelle Becker Slaton, Ph.D.

Poem, "Nelle's Stories: Repeating Tales."

Essay, "The Two Journeys of Biracial Identity" by Nelle Becker Slaton, Ph.D.

The poem "Around the World in Fitchburg" refers to the book, *Around the World in Fitchburg* (Volume II) by Doris Kirkpatrick, Fitchburg, Massachusetts: Fitchburg Historical Society, 1975.

Biography

Phyllis Becker coordinates the Riverfront Readings in Kansas City, Missouri, one of the longest-running literary reading series in the Midwest. She is also the author of *How I Came to Love Jazz and Other Poems* (Helicon Nine Editions) and the chapbook *Walking Naked into Sunday* (Wheel of Fire). Her work has been published in numerous venues, including *New Letters, I-70 Review, Worcester Review,* and *The Progressive* Her poems have also been set to jazz on the compact disc *Poetry of Love*, produced by jazz vocalist Angela Hagenbach. Becker also consults with organizations and communities in juvenile justice reform, community engagement, and professional development. She and her husband, Mark, are jazz enthusiasts and amateur gardeners.

www.ingramcontent.com/pod-product-compliance
Lightning Source LLC
Chambersburg PA
CBHW031427290426
44110CB00011B/560